Dreaming in the Night

How you rest, sleep and dream

Steve Parker

FRANKLIN WATTS
New York • London • Toronto • Sydney

© 1991 Franklin Watts

Franklin Watts, Inc.
387 Park Avenue South
New York, NY 10016

Library of Congress Cataloging-in-Publication Data
Parker, Steve.
    Dreaming in the night / Steve Parker.
      p.   cm. — (The Body in action)
    Summary: Examines dreaming as a neurological function and
describes in simple terms the length of dreams, their significance,
and the changes in the nervous system and the body during sleep.
    ISBN 0-531-14099-7
    1. Dreams—Juvenile literature.   2. Sleep—Physiological aspects—
Juvenile literature.   [1. Dreams.   2. Sleep.]   I. Title.
II. Series.
QP426.P37   1991
154.6′3—dc20   90-32396
                                                                     CIP AC

Printed in Great Britain

Medical consultant:
Dr. Puran Ganeri, MBBS, MRCP, MRCGP, DCH

Series editor: Anita Ganeri
Design: K and Co.
Illustrations: Hayward Art
Photography: Chris Fairclough
Typesetting: Lineage Ltd, Watford

The publisher would like to thank Lauren Bennett for
appearing in the photographs of this book.

CONTENTS

Getting tired

△ At a regular time each day, your body tells you that it needs to sleep by making you feel drowsy.

▷ As you grow from a baby into an adult, and then get older, your body follows a different daily routine. Young babies need much more sleep than children, who need more than adults. Some older people need less sleep than they did in middle age. However, each person is different. To an extent, you can "train" your body to need a bit more or less sleep.

Your body cannot stay active for too long. Many of its muscles and other parts get tired, and they need regular rest. You may spend time during the day sitting quietly or lying down. This helps your body to rest and relax. But your body's main period of rest is when you go to sleep. Sleep is especially important for your brain. If you try to stay awake for too long, your mind gets confused and you cannot think clearly. You also find it difficult to concentrate for very long.

Newborn baby's routine

2:00 am	sleeps
	wakes for feeding
4:00 am	sleeps
6:00 am	wakes and cries
	sleeps
8:00 am	wakes for feeding
10:00 am	sleeps
12:00 midday	wakes and lies quietly
	feeds
2:00 pm	sleeps
4:00 pm	wakes and feeds
6:00 pm	lies quietly
	sleeps
8:00 pm	wakes for feeding
10:00 pm	sleeps
12:00 midnight	wakes for feeding

SLEEP FACTS

- People's need for sleep varies depending on their age, what they do during the day, and how much sleep they are used to.
- In general, a newborn baby needs 16-20 hours of sleep a day.
- A six-year-old child needs up to 10 hours sleep a day.
- An average adult needs about 7-8 hours sleep a day.

- People who work at night, such as security guards, sleep during the day. Most prefer to sleep in the morning, rather than in the afternoon and evening.
- People who travel around the world to different time zones catch up on their sleep afterwards. Long-haul pilots may have several days off work, before their next flight.

	Schoolchild's routine	**Older person's routine**
2:00 am	sleeps	sleeps
4:00 am		wakes to go to bathroom
6:00 am		sleeps
8:00 am	wakes for breakfast	wakes for breakfast
10:00 am	morning at school	shopping
12:00 midday	lunchtime	
2:00 pm	afternoon at school	midday meal
	feels tired but not sleepy	nap after meal
4:00 pm	afternoon snack	afternoon walk
6:00 pm	sports	evening meal
	evening meal	
8:00 pm	bed and sleep	
10:00 pm		late-night television
12:00 midnight		bed and sleep

5

Ready for bed

At the end of the day, your body is tired – and probably dirty, too. Your skin may be covered with dust and dried sweat. You may have grime under your nails and bits of food stuck between your teeth. Most people follow a routine of washing up and brushing their teeth, before settling down for the night. This keeps your skin and mouth healthy.

△ Last thing at night is a good time to go to the bathroom and wash up, brush your teeth, and go to the toilet.

Brush up and down

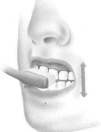

Brush in small circles

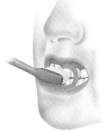

Brush from side to side

▷ If bits of old food stayed in your mouth, they would rot and damage your teeth and gums. Brush your teeth in different directions – up and down, from side to side, and in small circles. Clean the fronts and backs of the teeth, and try to reach every corner.

Clean the backs of your teeth, too

Reach right to the back of your back teeth

Rinse your mouth with clean water afterward

HYGIENE FACTS

- Your skin and hair grow all the time. Tiny flakes of skin rub off and hairs fall out regularly. If you could collect all this skin and hair over one year, it would weigh about 4½ pounds!
- Even though your skin is constantly being renewed, dirty skin, hair and nails all make it much easier for germs to grow and multiply.

- Dirty skin may be more likely to develop blackheads and pimples.
- Unwashed and unbrushed hair could become a home for tiny pests such as fleas, or lice and their eggs (called "nits").
- If you do not wash regularly, you and your clothes will smell of old sweat, and "body odor."

HOW WELL DOES SOAP WORK?

Soap helps to remove dirt and grime. It dissolves the grease and similar substances which hold particles of dirt, so that they can be carried away by water. Try some common substances to see which ones soap will remove. Some pens have water-soluble ink in them. Others are alcohol-soluble "permanent markers." What about the oil or grease? Even permanent ink disappears as the flakes of skin wear away.

water-soluble ink

permanent marker

oil-based grease

Settling down

At last, you are ready for sleep. Most of your body and brain become less active, but do not shut down. Nerve messages still go back and forth, and the brain sends out instructions to keep your heart beating and your lungs breathing. These tiny electrical signals spread "echoes" out from the brain, through the living tissue of your skull and skin. Doctors can detect these echoes by attaching delicate sensors, called electrodes, to the skin on your head.

△ Reading a book helps make you calm and relaxed, ready for sleep.

▷ All the time, even when you are sleeping deeply, electrical signals, called "brainwaves," flash around the brain. These can be detected by a machine, called an EEG machine. Below are the brainwaves of a person asleep and awake.

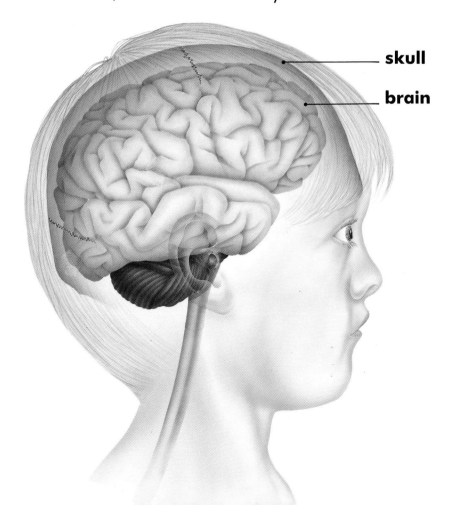

skull

brain

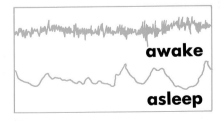

awake

asleep

8

CAN'T YOU GO TO SLEEP?

• Sometimes it is difficult to get to sleep. You may still feel alert and active, with your mind "racing" from the exciting events of the day. People use various tricks to help them calm down. Most involve simple, repeated thoughts that take your mind off other things.

• Think of waves lapping on the shore, one after the other.

• Imagine sheep jumping over a fence. You don't have to count them all!

• Try to identify, and then ignore, noises that keep you awake, such as water pipes gurgling in the house or tree leaves rustling. Once you know what the noises are, they will be less of a problem.

LEARNING TO RELAX

If your muscles are tense, try these relaxation techniques to help you get to sleep. Lie on your back, with your legs straight out and your eyes lightly closed. Start with your head and face. Screw your face up hard. Then relax your face so that you can feel no tightness in the muscles. Can you feel the tension being smoothed away? Now clench your fists tightly, then unclench them slowly and relax the tensed-up muslces. Do this for every part of your body, right down to your toes. Tense up each part, then relax it slowly and smoothly. Now concentrate on your breathing. Breathe slowly and regularly ... Goodnight!

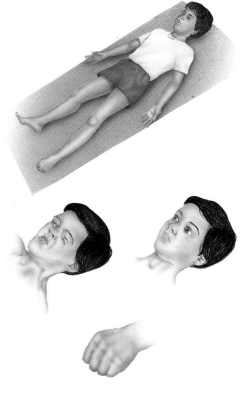

Falling asleep

As you fall asleep, your body's activities slow down, so that you do not have to keep getting up to eat, have a drink or use the bathroom during the night. If your kidneys made urine at the same rate as during the day, you would have to get up two or three times in the night to empty your bladder!

△ A comfortable bed with warm covers helps you to sleep.
To keep warm, you may curl up in a position like this one. ▽

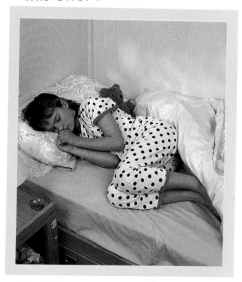

▷ Many parts of your body slow down at night.

Lungs breathe more slowly and regularly

Heartbeat becomes slower and more regular

Muscles relax and need less blood

Kidneys make less urine, which trickles into your bladder for storage

SYSTEMS FACTS

- Your body uses less energy when it is asleep. Your muscles are relaxed, and your digestive system and other internal parts slow down.
- This means your body needs less oxygen and energy. These are supplied by the blood. So your heart can pump blood more sluggishly around the body. Its beating rate may fall by 10-20 beats a minute, to 60 beats a minute or even less.
- Your breathing slows down too. At night, you breathe about 105-140 cubic feet of air. This is about the volume needed to inflate a very, very large balloon.
- Your breathing and heartbeat are controlled by the lowest part of your brain, called the medulla. It keeps your body's basic life processes going.

BREATHING SLOWLY

As you fall asleep, your breathing becomes more shallow. You do not breathe as deeply as you do when you are awake, so you take in less air with each breath. Your breathing also slows down. It is difficult to test this on yourself. Your breathing rate will automatically go up as you concentrate on the test. But you can test it on a brother, sister or friend.

Before they go to bed, use a watch to count the number of times they breathe in one minute. Try not to make it too obvious that you are watching them. Watch how many times their chest rises and falls. Let them settle into bed and relax for a few minutes. Then count their breaths again. Compare this with their breathing rate before they get into bed. What is the difference? You could even try this on a pet dog or cat.

Deep sleep

When you sleep, your body does not stay still until you wake next morning. Every so often, you move and change position (see page 14). Neither does your brain activity stay the same. Scientists studying the "brainwaves" of sleeping people have shown that the brain goes through a cycle of deep sleep, when it is difficult to be woken, and then shallow sleep, when you are more likely to wake up. This cycle happens several times each night. Each cycle lasts about 90 minutes.

△ About half an hour after you drop off, you are in very deep sleep. This is when it is most difficult to wake up.

▽ Your brain goes through several cycles of deep sleep, and then shallow, or light, sleep. Toward morning the deep sleep becomes less deep. You are more likely to be woken by a noise, by being cold because the blankets have fallen off, or by some other disturbance.

sleep cycle

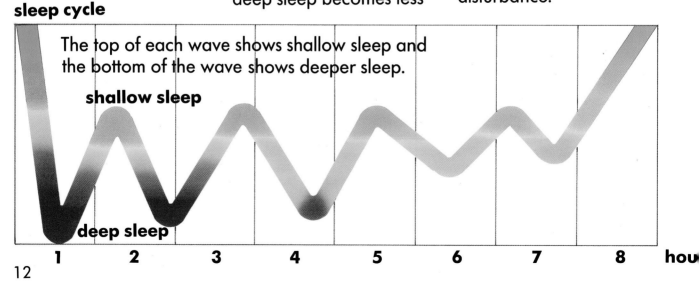

The top of each wave shows shallow sleep and the bottom of the wave shows deeper sleep.

shallow sleep

deep sleep

1   2   3   4   5   6   7   8   hou

SNORING FACTS

- Some people make snoring and snorting noises when asleep. Often, this does not wake them up, but it can be very annoying for others nearby!
- The snoring noise is made by the rattling of the soft palate. This is the flap at the back of the roof of the mouth, where the mouth connects to the nose. Air passes back and forth through your mouth as you breathe and makes the flap vibrate.
- You are more likely to snore if you lie on your back, or if you have a bad cold and your nose is full of mucus (congestion).
- To stop someone from snoring, turn them on to their side, and gently close their mouth. You can stop yourself from snoring by using more pillows.

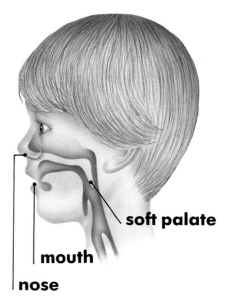

soft palate

mouth

nose

TWITCH AND BRUSH

Even when you are fast asleep, many of your body's automatic reactions still protect you from possible harm. If a fly lands on your face, you may twitch the muscles there, or brush it away with your hand. You can do this without waking up. You can test these reactions by lying down, with your eyes closed, pretending to be asleep. Ask a friend to tickle your face with a feather or a tissue. See how difficult it is not to twitch, and not to brush the feather or tissue away from you.

MOVING IN THE NIGHT

During the night, without waking up, you regularly move an arm or leg, or even turn right over. You may do this 30 or more times each night. These movements help to prevent parts of your body from becoming too squashed or bent and having their blood supply cut off. You can find out more about this below.

WHAT HAPPENS WHEN YOUR ARM "GOES TO SLEEP?"

If you sit or lie in the same position for too long when you are awake, parts of your body may "go to sleep." The blood vessels and nerves become squashed, causing a tingling and then an aching feeling. This warns you to relieve the pressure, so you move the part into a new position. You then feel "pins and needles" as the nerves expand to normal and the blood flow returns.

The same happens when you really are asleep. It occurs automatically, as you can see above.

You can test this by sitting with your arm resting on a hard, thin surface, such as the wooden arm of a chair. The chair arm presses about halfway along your forearm. After a few minutes your arm and hand may start to feel uncomfortable. You soon need to move your arm. Do not ignore this — it is one of the body's many built-in safety features.

Dreaming

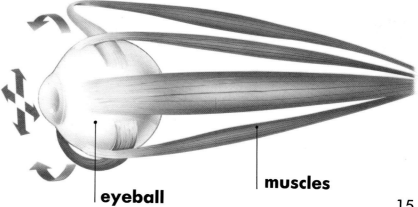

△ Dreams often have links with real life. You may dream about a movie you saw, or an exciting event you heard about. Yet facts are mixed up with fantasy in a strange way.

▷ REM means Rapid Eye Movement. This is the type of shallow sleep when your eyes flick back and forth. People woken during REM sleep usually say they have been dreaming. On the right you can see the muscles that move your eyes during REM sleep.

Do you often have dreams? During shallow sleep, your brain has bursts of activity, as shown by its brainwaves. Also, your eyes may move quickly, as though you are looking around at different things. Your breathing and heartbeat become more irregular. Yet you are still asleep, with your eyelids closed. It is thought that dreams occur when all this activity takes place.

eyeball

muscles

SLEEPTALKING AND SLEEPWALKING

No one fully understands why some people talk or walk in their sleep. This usually happens during very deep sleep, when the brainwaves show a pattern known as delta waves. If you sleeptalk, you probably mumble quickly, and the words do not make much sense to a listener. If you sleepwalk, you may try to go to the bathroom, or you may just wander about. Often, sleeptalking or sleepwalking are linked to real events that have happened recently, which are important to you. These events, like an exam at school or an argument, may be worrying you or may be stuck at the back of your mind.

can't remember

DREAM FACTS

• Almost everyone dreams, every night. But most of us cannot remember our dreams when we wake up, so we do not think we have dreamed.
• Most dreams occur during REM sleep. Of people woken during REM sleep, four out of five say that they have been dreaming.
• Woken during deep sleep, only about two out of five people can remember they have been dreaming.
• Dreaming can last up to one hour, although you might have several different dreams during this time.
• You mainly dream in pictures. But these often seem to fade into black and white, rather than being in color.
• Dreaming seems to be an essential part of sleep. People woken as soon as they start REM sleep show confused thinking more often than people woken during deep sleep.
• When allowed to sleep again, these people catch up on their lost REM sleep rather than on their deep sleep.

CAN YOU REMEMBER YOUR DREAMS?

Unless you wake in the middle of a dream or just after, you probably won't remember much about it. If you want to recall your dreams, try the following experiment. Since you probably dream more towards the morning, set your alarm clock slightly earlier than normal. Have a pencil and paper ready by your bed to write down any memories you have of the dream. You will also need to remind yourself to recall your dream, since you may forget during the night. So write a note to yourself and put this in front of your alarm clock, where you are bound to see it as soon as you wake up. Once you start to recall a dream and write it down, you will probably remember more and more about it.

WHAT DO DREAMS MEAN?

There are many ideas about what dreams mean, and whether they could be important to real life. Your brain may be filtering through the happenings of the past few days, and trying to deal with problems or think through puzzling events. Or it may be trying to make sense of random nerve messages that occur in its various parts during sleep. Common subjects for dreams include falling, flying, taking a test, losing something, chasing or being chased. You may dream you are falling if you are worried about problems which have not been solved, but should have been.

Noises in the night

While you sleep, your body is not cut off from the outside world. Your ears and nose, especially, are on the alert and sending messages to your brain. The sleeping brain ignores most of the messages, but if an important one comes through, it recognizes this, and you may wake up. Especially important are messages which could warn of danger, such as someone crying out, the smell of smoke, or your body being moved or jolted.

△ In the still of the night, even a small noise may seem loud and startling.

▷ Your ears detect sound waves, which are vibrations in the air. The waves hit your eardrum, which vibrates in turn. It sends the vibrations along three tiny bones to the snail-shaped cochlea deep inside the ear. Here they are changed into electrical nerve signals and sent to your brain.

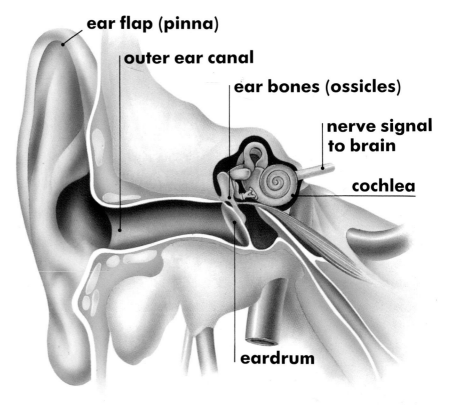

ear flap (pinna)

outer ear canal

ear bones (ossicles)

nerve signal to brain

cochlea

eardrum

NIGHT-NOISE FACTS

- Your ears adjust to the general level of sounds. If you are near a jet plane, they become less sensitive, so that they are not damaged by the loud roar of the engines.
- In the quiet of the night, your ears are very sensitive to sounds. They detect softer noises than they can during the noisy hubbub of the day.
- You soon get used to noises which you hear regularly, such as the sound of a dripping tap, the hum of electrical equipment, or the rattle of windows. These do not usually wake you.
- Any unusual or out-of-place sound, such as the squeal of fighting cats, is more likely to rouse you from sleep.
- More gentle, smoother sounds, such as an owl's hoot, may not wake you — even if they are as loud as the cat's screech.
- If a familiar sound suddenly stops, like a ticking clock, this may wake you, too!

SLEEPING SOMEWHERE ELSE

You probably find it difficult to get to sleep when you are staying somewhere else. There are often new, strange sounds, which keep you from falling asleep. This often happens when camping, with only a thin layer of canvas to keep out sounds. Next time you stay away from home, keep a sleep diary. Ask a grown-up to make a note of when you fall asleep each evening. Keep a record of the time you wake up each morning. Do you gradually get used to the new noises and surroundings, and sleep longer each night?

COMING TO YOUR SENSES

As soon as you wake up, your eyes open and your brain becomes more alert. You may feel slightly dazed, especially if you were in the deep sleep part of one of the sleep cycles. If it is still dark, you may not be able to see well, but unless it is almost complete darkness, your eyes soon become adjusted (see page 24). Swiftly your body systems begin to speed up, ready for action. Your senses collect information about your surroundings, and your brain tries to figure out what made the noise that woke you up.

HEARING THINGS

Tiny electrical nerve signals from your ear travel along the main nerve, called the auditory nerve, to a special part of your brain. This is called the hearing center. It receives and sorts out the nerve signals, so that you can try to identify the sudden sound you heard.

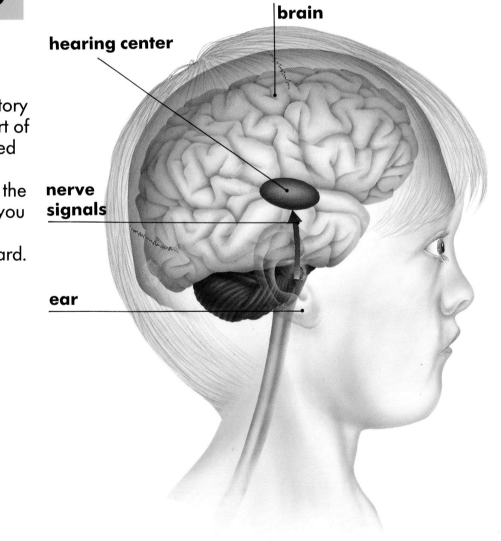

brain

hearing center

nerve signals

ear

20

Ready for action

△ Wide awake by now, you put on a light to check that the room is safe. Your eyes soon adjust to the light (see page 24).

When you are worried or frightened, changes take place in your body. Your muscles become tense, your heart beats faster, and you may begin to pant. These changes prepare you for action. They are caused by nerve signals, and also by a natural body chemical called adrenaline.

▷ Adrenaline is a type of body chemical called a hormone (see page 22). It is made in two adrenal glands, one on top of each kidney. As it travels around in your blood, adrenaline gets your body ready for action — such as running away!

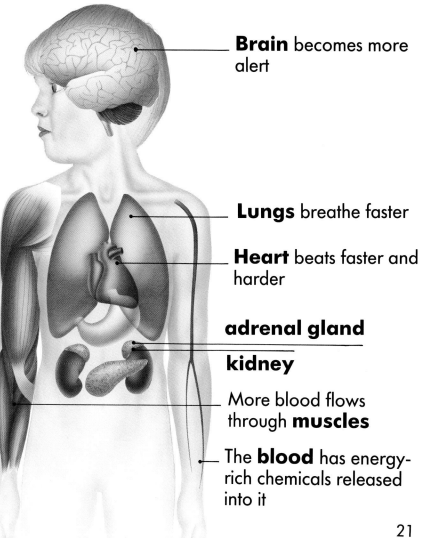

Brain becomes more alert

Lungs breathe faster

Heart beats faster and harder

adrenal gland

kidney

More blood flows through **muscles**

The **blood** has energy-rich chemicals released into it

HORMONE FACTS

- Hormones are body chemicals made in special organs, which are called hormonal or endocrine glands.
- The hormones spread around in your blood. Each affects different parts of your body, called target organs.
- The pituitary is your body's "master gland." It is a pea-sized gland just below your brain. It makes eight hormones which control other hormone-making glands, as well as making other hormones of its own.
- These include growth hormone, which affects how fast you grow. More growth hormone is produced at night, as you sleep.
- Too much growth hormone makes someone grow much faster and taller than normal. Too little makes a person grow much more slowly and smaller than normal.

HORMONES IN YOUR BLOOD

The amount of hormone in your blood depends on a "feedback loop." You can see how this works by half-filling a sink with water. Tilt the stopper slightly and turn on the tap a little, so that equal amounts of water pour in and drain away. Add a few drops of food coloring to the water, and stir. The coloring is like a hormone released into the blood. It stains the water, but the color soon fades as some of the coloring goes down the drain. This is like your body using a hormone. Add more coloring, trying to keep the same amount of color in the water. You are acting as the "feedback loop." As the color fades you add more coloring; as it darkens you add less to keep the color fairly constant.

color fades

color darkens

Back to sleep

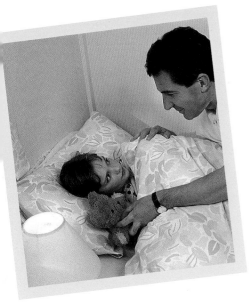

At last, the mystery of the strange noise is solved. It was simply a car honking its horn on the new road built nearby. However, it is difficult for you to relax right away. It takes some minutes for the effects of the adrenaline to wear off, as it is gradually used up from the bloodstream. Eventually you settle again, as your heart stops thumping and your breathing slows down.

△ Being tucked in after a fright makes you feel safer and calmer. The danger is over and your body settles down. You soon feel tired again.

▷ Adrenaline works with your brain and nerves to coordinate your reaction to fright, worry or stress. The result is the "fight or flight" reaction. It helps your body to get ready for possible danger, and either to stay and fight or to flee from it.

Hair on head and neck stands on end

Eye pupils open wide

Tiny hairs on skin stand up, giving goose pimples

Blood vessels in skin narrow, so your skin turns paler

Heart beats faster

Lungs breathe faster

Stomach gets "butterflies"

SLEEPLESSNESS FACTS

- Lack of sleep can make you tired, bad-tempered, slow to react, more likely to fall ill, and unable to concentrate.
- Problems in sleeping are one of the most common causes of people visiting the doctor.
- Difficulty in sleeping is called insomnia.
- People who can stay healthy on only one or two hours' sleep each night are called nonsomniacs.
- Narcolepsy is a rare condition in which the person suddenly falls asleep, anywhere and at any time.
- Sleeplessness is often caused by problems or worries at school or at work.

CAN YOU SEE IN THE DARK?

Your eyes adjust themselves to different levels of light just as your ears adjust to different levels of sound. The pupil, the black-looking hole in the middle of your eye, can become bigger or smaller. In the dark, it widens to let in more light. It shrinks to keep out too much light when it is very bright. Ask a friend to cover her or his eyes for a minute or so, so their eyes are in the dark. When their eyes are uncovered, the pupils will be large. Within a second or two they narrow, as they adjust to the brighter light level.

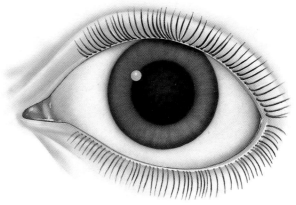

wide pupil in dim light

narrow pupil in bright light

MORE HORMONES

Here are some more examples of hormonal glands. Adrenaline is one of the faster-acting hormones, giving effects in seconds. Other hormones are slower acting over many weeks or months.

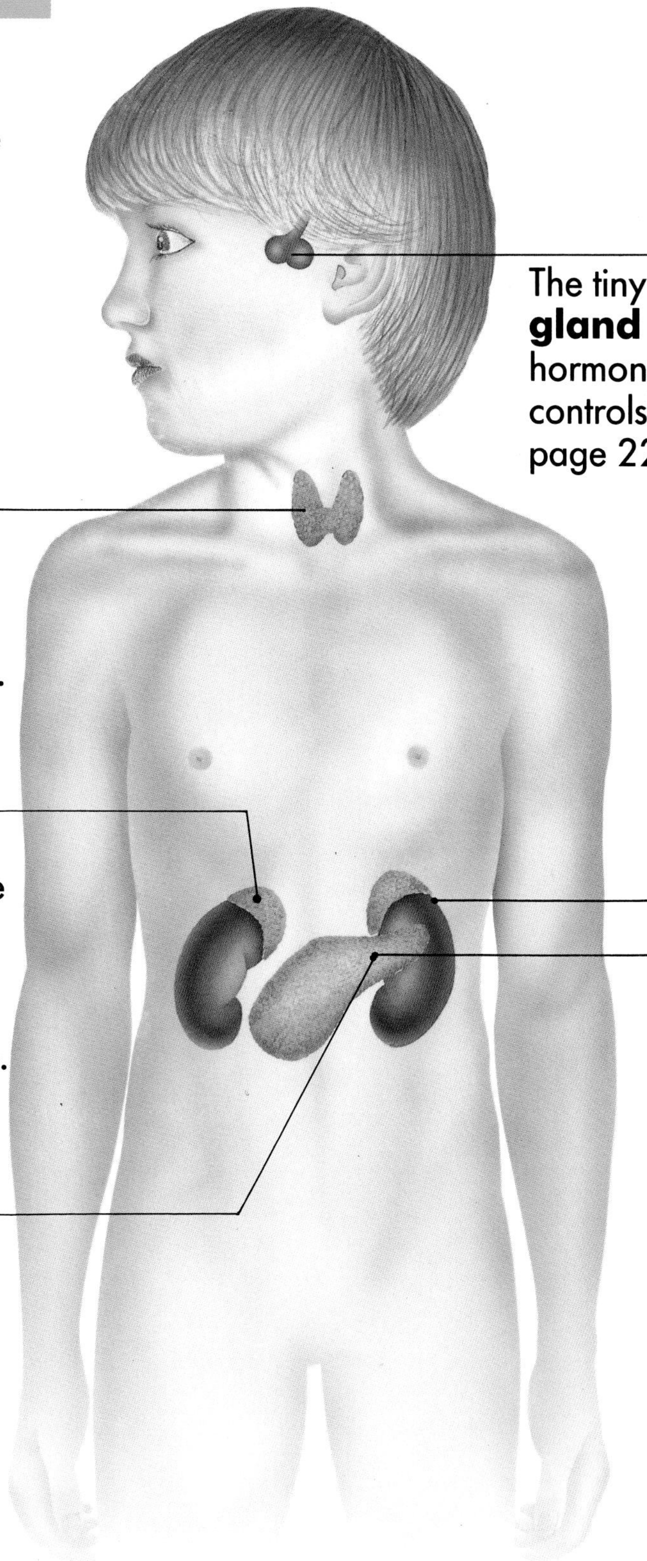

The **thyroid gland** in your neck makes thyroxine, which speeds up many body processes.

Besides adrenaline, the **adrenal glands** make a hormone called aldosterone. It controls how much salt the kidneys get rid of in urine.

Your **pancreas** just below your stomach makes insulin, which controls the use of energy by many body parts.

The tiny **pituitary gland** makes its own hormones and also controls other glands (see page 22).

kidney

pancreas

25

Good morning!

At last, your body has had enough sleep. During the night it has been using up energy and nutrients, to repair worn-out parts and to build new ones to make you grow. It has also been slowly making urine and you may need to use the bathroom. You also need to take in new supplies of energy and nutrients by eating breakfast.

△ As you wake up, you bend your joints and stretch your muscles. This helps to get them working gradually, so that you do not strain them by moving them too suddenly.

▷ Daytime needs gradually take over from nighttime ones as you get up and move about. Your brain becomes more alert as your senses detect the sights, sounds, smells, tastes and touches of the new day.

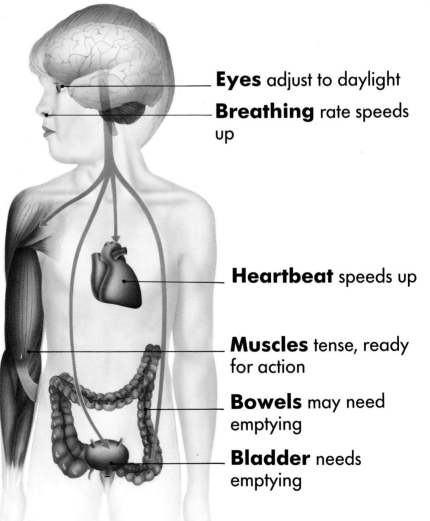

Eyes adjust to daylight

Breathing rate speeds up

Heartbeat speeds up

Muscles tense, ready for action

Bowels may need emptying

Bladder needs emptying

26

BODY CLOCK FACTS

- The human body has a "built-in" clock which gives a daily rhythm of activity, resting, eating and sleeping.
- This rhythm is kept in time with the outside world by daily changes such as sunlight and darkness, heat and cold.
- Yet research on people living in constant conditions, with none of these outside changes, shows

that they still follow a routine of about 22-27 hours — because of the body clock.
- Sometimes this

internal clock falls out of sync with the outside world. People who fly halfway around the world find themselves in broad daylight, while their body clock says it is time for bed!
- This can cause problems such as jet lag. The sufferer is tired and has dulled senses, is slow to respond, has headaches and feels sick, and may even tremble and feel giddy.

WAKE-UP CHECKLIST

- Try to write down a list of the things you do each morning soon after you wake up. Do you stretch, yawn, blink or scratch? How do they help your body get ready for the day ahead?
- Yawning opens up the air passages in your lungs and stretches your chest and neck muscles, ready for deeper breathing. It also helps to get more

oxygen into your blood, and gets rid of waste gases in your body.
- You may scratch to remove a piece of fluff or a bent-over hair that is irritating your skin.
- Ask your friends to keep their own wake-up diaries, too.

Things to do

TOO HOT OR COLD?

To sleep properly, your body must be kept at a comfortable temperature. Its own internal temperature is lowest between 2:00 and 5:00, in the early morning. But if you have too many or not enough blankets, you may get too hot or cold, and so wake up. Try going to sleep with two or three extra blankets on your bed. You may soon find yourself pushing or kicking them off, as your body senses that it is becoming too hot.

SLEEP SURVEY

Organize a survey of sleeping habits among your family, friends or classmates. Ask questions such as what time they go to bed, when they usually fall asleep, when they wake up, and what time they get out of bed. Draw a chart or graph of the results, and figure out the average sleep time for different age groups. Do you find that most people have very similar sleeping times? Or is there a wide range of times?

	Age	Sleep
John	1	15
Grandad	60	8
Bob	6	10

HELPFUL SWEAT

Sweat may make you feel sticky and uncomfortable, but it has many uses. It helps to cool your body when you become too hot. It also helps you to grip! Put a fine needle or pin on a flat surface. Try to pick it up with your finger and thumb. This is probably quite easy. Now wash your hands well with warm water and soap, and dry them thoroughly on a clean towel, to get rid of all traces of sweat and oil. Try again to pick up the needle. It is probably more difficult. The fine film of sweat on your fingertips helps you to grasp small objects.

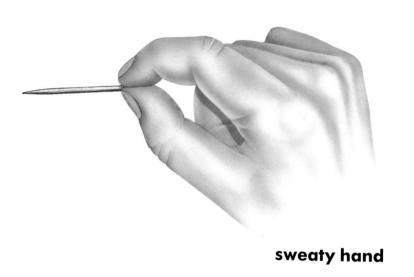

sweaty hand

DAY AND NIGHT ANIMALS

Most animals are active in the daytime, like people. They are called "diurnal." But some animals are called "nocturnal," which means they are out and about at night. Some nocturnal animals have big eyes, to help them see in the dark. Others have huge ears to pick up faint sounds, and large whiskers to feel their way. Some even have a radar sound-system to navigate in the darkness. Try to find out about these night animals. Begin with bats, owls and mice. What about cats, snails, worms and cockroaches?

Glossary

Adrenaline A hormone that prepares the body for action, by the "fight or flight" reaction.

Brain A large, tangled mass of tissue and interconnected nerve cells inside the head. It is the control center of the body. Other nerves link it to the various body parts.

Center In the brain, a part that is specialized to deal with nerve messages coming in from, or going out to, a certain part of the body. For example, the hearing center deals with nerve messages coming from the ear.

Cochlea A snail-shaped body part deep in the ear, which turns vibrations into nerve signals and sends them to the brain.

Dream Pictures and ideas experienced by the brain when you are asleep.

EEG A machine which detects brainwaves, the tiny electrical nerve signals inside the brain. It is called an Electroencephalograph.

Hormone A body chemical made by a hormonal, or endocrine gland, which is released into the blood and affects certain parts of the body.

Hygiene Keeping the body clean, avoiding dirt and germs. Hygiene can also apply to clothes, food, and anything else that comes into contact with the body.

Insomnia Difficulty in getting a good night's sleep.

Kidneys Parts of the body which filter waste substances and excess water from the blood, to make watery urine.

Muscle Part of the body that can contract, or get shorter. As it does so it pulls on other parts, such as bones or other muscles, and moves them.

Nerve A long, thin bundle of neurons (nerve cells) that carries nerve messages from one part of the body to another.

Nerve message A series of tiny bursts of electricity that travel along a nerve, like a series of electrical signals going along a telephone wire.

Pituitary The body's "master hormonal gland," which makes its own hormones and also controls other hormonal glands. It is attached to the lower portion of the brain, in the bone at the back of the roof of the mouth.

REM sleep Rapid Eye Movement sleep, when the eyes flick around under closed lids. Most dreams happen during REM sleep.

Sense organ A part of the body that detects some aspect of its surroundings, turns it into electrical nerve messages, and sends these to the brain. The eye does this with light rays.

Sleep cycle A period of deep, or heavy, sleep, followed by shallow, or light, sleep, which happens several times each night.

Target organ The part of the body affected by a hormone.

Resources

United States Government Printing Office
Superintendent of Documents
Washington, D.C. 20402

(Request leaflets on health and fitness)

BOOKS

***The Human Body* by Linda Gamlin.**
New York; Gloucester Press, 1988.

***Sleeping and Dreaming* by R. Milos.**
Chicago; Children's Press, 1987.

***The Brain and Nervous System* by Steve Parker.**
New York; Franklin Watts, 1990.

***The Human Body and How it Works* by Angela Royston.**
New York; Warwick, 1991.

Index